The Kettlebell Swing
Amazingly Simple, but Extremely Detailed

Your first step to becoming a serious Kettleb...
Improve your cardiovascular endurance and pote...

This book covers every intrinsic detail of the kettlebell swing, explained and broken down in such a way that everyone can understand it; it's basic but at the same time advanced.

"The most comprehensive guide on the Kettlebell Swing I have ever seen." ~ *Derek Fronczak (NESTA Certified Personal Fitness Trainer and Functional Training specialist)*

"This book is a must for kettlebell enthusiasts and crossfitters looking to learn how to swing efficienctly, safely and correctly." ~ *Anna Junghans (Kettlebell Trainer and owner of Gym Elite)*

Published by Cavemantraining and written by Taco Fleur

The Conventional Two Arm Kettlebell Swing (Hip Hinge Style)

If at this point in time you have not read the Ebook, *"What is the Hip Hinge? How do You Perform it Correctly? Explained in plain English so everyone can understand it,"* I strongly suggest you do so, as it's a precursor to the Kettlebell Swing. It is available for purchase on Amazon*, on Cavemantraining** bundled with the Audiobook, or delivered with Kettlebell Courses at www.cavemantraining.com. We decided to separate the details on the hip hinge from this book as it allows us to keep the price of this book down, let people decide what they want to learn and how deep they want their knowledge on this subject to be. We've included enough information on the hip hinge to fully understand the kettlebell swing.

www.cavemantraining.com

kettlebelltraining.education

www.tacofleur.com

Table of Contents

Taco Fleur

WARNING: To reduce risk of injury, in your case, consult your health professional before attempting an exercise that is covered in this document. The instructions and advice presented are in no way intended as substitute for medical counselling. The creators, producers, participants and distributors of this program disclaim any liabilities for loss in connection with the exercises and advice herein. The author disclaims an responsibility from any adverse effects or consequences from the misapplication or injurious use of information presented.

BEGINNERS: An overload of information might shut you down, therefore it's important to create yourself strategy to learn from this book. It might be that you read the whole book, then start with the most importan points, which are; the hip hinge, pendulum concept and explosiveness. From there you might progress to adding points that you want to work on bit by bit. Whatever the case, you'll probably want to be referrin back to this book over and over again until you feel that you have mastered the swing.

ASSESSMENT: This book will provide you with everything you need to know about the kettlebell swing but unfortunately it can't provide you with an assessment of your swing, therefore we have created an online discussion group for questions, when you're ready, create your account and post your kettlebell swing vide for assessment from kettlebell trainers. If you mention this book, you might even get assessed by the Autho himself. www.facebook.com/groups/kettlebell.swing/

Introduction

The Kettlebell swing is a full-body exercise that can be performed with one or two arms. We are going to cover the two-arm conventional swing.

Kettlebell exercises can be categorized into three categories, Ballistic, Hybrid and Grinding Exercises. Any variation of the kettlebell swing is a ballistic exercise, meaning it's a dynamic, explosive and multi-joint exercise. The opposite of a ballistic exercise is a grinding exercise, an example of a grinding but very closely related exercise is the Hip Hinge Deadlift. An example of a hybrid exercise would be the Kettlebell squat thruster, where the squatting can be grinding and the thrust is ballistic.

The Kettlebell Swing movement is very similar to that of the Conventional Deadlift. The main difference is that the weight swings and the movement is explosive; the hinge movement of the hips is the same.

When the Kettlebell Swing is mentioned, it's usually the Conventional Two Arm Kettlebell Swing (also known as the Russian Swing) that is being referred to. The second most-popular swing is the American Swing. The least popular swing is the Swing Squat Style.

The Kettlebell Swing is the foundation for many other Kettlebell exercises. Therefore, it is important you become proficient in this exercise and understand all the finer points.

The Kettlebell Swing is the foundation for:

- Single-arm swing
- Swing clean
- Snatch

Swing Variations

Lets address something extremely important right away and avoid any confusion. There are many variations of the swing, but within each swing variation there are also a hundred and one ways to perform each of those kettlebell swing variations. Our Caveman Kettlebell swing explanation is all about safety, cleanliness, trajectory, control, resistance and adding as many muscle groups as possible. This is our way of swinging a Kettlebell, but that doesn't mean that the other ways are incorrect or our way is superior, in the end it's all about context and goals. Your choice. If you're doing the Kettlebell Swing for strength, cardio and flexibility, then you'd rather be doing a swing version that employs as many muscles as possible, is effective and safe.

Some variations are timing of the hip hinge and even depth of the hip hinge, with our variation of the swing we want to provide as much resistance as possible but keep it safe, this means that we can vary the timing of the hip hinge, but we recommend not to perform hinge at the same moment the bell starts the down-phase but employ a slight delay before hinging at the hips. The delay is anywhere from 5° to 40° of the full motion, where 0° would be the top of the swing, this delay is important to prevent a compromised position of the lower-back, the more you delay the hip hinge, the less resistance is provided to the back and muscles that keep the spine erect. If you break too early, then the kettlebell runs the risk of coming out of the safe trajectory, not only can this create unbalanced weight but can also puts unnecessary pressure on the lower-back and potential for the heels being pulled off the ground to counter-balance.

Illustrated: hip hinge delay

ollowing is a list of Kettlebell Swing variations. This information is taken from the omplete list of all kettlebell exercises and can be found on the Cavemantraining website: avemantraining.com/caveman-kettlebells/list-kettlebell-exercises/

- **Conventional Swing** AKA Russian Swing, Hip Hinge Style
  - ☐ Single-Arm (one kettlebell)
  - ☐ Single-Arm Alternating (one kettlebell)
  - ☐ Double-Arm (one kettlebell)
  - ☐ Double-Arm (two kettlebells)

- **Squat Style Swing**
  - ☐ Single-Arm (one kettlebell)
  - ☐ Single-Arm Alternating (one kettlebell)
  - ☐ Double-Arm (one kettlebell)
  - ☐ Double-Arm(two kettlebells)

- **American Swing**

Taco Fleur

-     ☐ Double-Arm (one kettlebell)

- **Kettlebell Sport Swing**
  - ☐ Single-Arm (one kettlebell)
  - ☐ Single-Arm Alternating (one kettlebell)

- **Short Lever Swing**
  - ☐ Double-Arm (one kettlebell)

- **Side Swing**
  - ☐ Single-Arm (one kettlebells)
  - ☐ Double-Arm (two kettlebells)

- **Walking Swing**
  - ☐ Single-Arm (one kettlebell)
  - ☐ Double-Arm (one kettlebell)
  - ☐ Double-Arm (two kettlebells)

- **Reverse Walking Swing**
  - ☐ Single-Arm (one kettlebell)
  - ☐ Double-Arm (one kettlebell)
  - ☐ Double-Arm (two kettlebells)

- **Swing High Pull**
  - ☐ Single-Arm (one kettlebells)
  - ☐ Double-Arm (two kettlebells)

- **Power Swing**
  - ☐ Double-Arm (one kettlebell)

With kettlebell training in most cases you want resistance, in kettlebell sport you'll always want to reduce resistance and be as efficient as possible, meaning delay of the hip hinge, less depth, more squat and remaining more upright.

The following link provides more information about kettlebell training vs kettlebell sport

www.cavemantraining.com/caveman-kettlebells/kb-training-vs-kettlebell-sport-answers-youve-looking/

This is a good time to define the hip hinge and squat movement, let's start with the squat.

Cavemantraining Definition of the Squat

Movement

- Torso remaining as much as possible in the vertical plane
- Hips always moving down in the vertical plane

Hinge joints

- Hips
- Knees
- Ankles

A squat is performed in standing position with the objective being to move the hip joints as close to the ground as possible, this is achieved through flexion in 3 joints; flexion in the hip joints, flexion in the knee joints; and dorsiflexion in the ankle joints.

If flexion is achieved in any of the joints that define the squat, but no maximum depth achieved, then it's further defined by the approximate height; quarter squat; half squat; three-quarter squat; where as maximum depth would be a full squat. A quick quarter squat can also be defined as a dip.

The objective of the squat exercise is to tax the quadriceps and gluteus maximus. A completely vertical position of the torso provides the maximum resistance for the quadriceps, and the more it moves towards the horizontal plane, the more it removes resistance from the target muscles. Furthermore, a vertical position of the torso provides the most stable and safe spinal structure for the weighted squat. The torso should never break the angle of 45° flexion.

Cavemantraining Definition of the Hip Hinge

Movement
- Torso moving towards but never past the horizontal plane
- Hips remaining in horizontal plane, or moving backwards and down in the vertical plane, but never breaking the angle of 45° flexion

Hinge joints
- Fixed: hips
- Variable: knees

A hip hinge is performed in standing position with the objective being to move the torso towards the horizontal plane, this is achieved through flexion in the hip joints. The movement can (variable) also be accompanied by flexion in a second joint, that of the knees, which is cause for the hips to move down and backwards. The function of added knee flexion is to create a more balanced weight distribution, especially with weighted hip hinges like deadlifts.

If the ankle joints move and dorsiflexion is achieved, then the definition of the movement changes to a squat.

The objective of the hip hinge exercise is to tax the gluteus maximus and hamstrings (hip extensors). A completely horizontal torso provides the maximum resistance for the hip flexors, and the more it moves towards the vertical plane, the more resistance is removed.

The maximum recommend hip flexion is 45° for weighted hip hinges.

For more intricate details on the hip hinge buy our book.

Squatting Versus Hip Hinging

There is a lot of controversy about people performing a squat movement rather than a hip hinge movement when swinging a Kettlebell. I have written a whole article* about this online. In summation: When you're performing the conventional kettlebell swing (the hip hinge style swing) you should be hip hinging and not squatting. However, there is also a squat style of the kettlebell swing, and this version is not bad when performed correctly; it simply works different muscle groups.

When does a hip hinge turn into a squat? The movement turns into a squat once the knees move forward towards or past the knees (involving the ankle joints), the hips are moving down rather than back, the torso remains more upright, the load moves more towards the quads and the movement is now additionally powered by the quads.

Pre-requisites and Progression

To progress to the Kettlebell swing the following pre-requisites and progressions must be met.

- You should have a sound understanding of the bodyweight hip hinge and be able to perform this movement.

Taco Fleur

- You should have a sound understanding of the Pendulum Concept, as this plus added resistance and explosiveness is the main difference between a bodyweight hip hinge and a kettlebell swing.

In a perfect world you would progress yourself or your clients as follows:

1. Bodyweight Hip Hinge
2. Kettlebell 3HL (hip hinge hang lift, less flexibility required)
3. Kettlebell Conventional Deadlift (more flexibility required)
4. Kettlebell Swing

Posture

Good posture with every swing is important to avoid injury, generate maximum power and be able to perform high reps. A good posture is standing straight with a neutral spine pulling your shoulders back and down (packed) to keep the load off the shoulders and neck. Doing so will place most of the load on the scapula and lats. Improper form will result in smaller muscles needing to do the work, rather than the larger and stronger muscles groups, thus creating potential for injury.

Muscles Involved

The Kettlebell swing is a full body exercise and helps to strengthen the posterior chain muscles.

The posterior chain muscles are comprised of various muscles. The main muscle groups are: biceps femoris; glutes; erector spinae; trapezius; posterior deltoids; rhomboids soleus; and latissimus dorsi.

When performed correctly, the Kettlebell swing will involve the following muscles and muscle groups: gluteus maximus; biceps femoris; erector spinae; trapezius; and latissimus dorsi.

For grips, the following muscles are involved: flexor digitorum superficialis; flexor digitorum profondus; and the flexor policus longus, which are muscles located in the posterior part of the forearm.

The following muscles are involved to create a proper pivot for the pendulum: trapezius; latissimus dorsi; and rhomboids.

The gluteus maximus powers the hip hinge.

Assisting muscles for the hip hinge include the biceps femoris and erector spinae.

The latissimus dorsi muscles should be engaged as much as possible to keep the shoulders down and create a tight posture which has more control over the movement.

The trapezius muscles are more involved on the down phase of the swing, as the force of the weight is pulling the shoulders down and the trapezius needs to be engaged to pull them up.

The biceps femoris are involved with knee flexion and also involved in hip extension.

Muscle Groups

The Rhomboids are a muscle group consisting of Rhomboid Minor and Rhomboid Major.

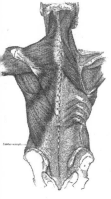

Taco Fleur

The Glutes are a muscle group consisting of Gluteus Maximus, Gluteus Minimum and Gluteus Medius.

Glutes AKA Gluteal Muscles

The Erector Spinae are a muscle group consisting of **Iliocostalis**, Longissimus and Spinalis.

Erector Spinae AKA Spinal Erectors

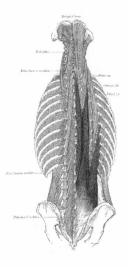

Phases of the Kettlebell Swing

The Kettlebell Swing has four phases to the movement

    1. Top or floating phase. The kettlebell floats in the air and appears weightless for a

split second

2. **Down phase**. The kettlebell falls back down as gravity pulls it down

3. **End phase**. The kettlebell has reached the end of the swing and is hanging from the arms, ready be pulled back up

4. **Up phase**. The kettlebell is propelled back up

Pendulum Concept

It is important to understand the concept of a pendulum because this is what the arms will be acting as during the swing. A pendulum is a weight suspended from a pivot so that it can swing freely.

A great drill to teach the concept of the pendulum is to ask the participant to perform the static hang phase of the hip hinge with a light kettlebell. Have the participant pull their shoulders back, chest out, let the arms hang loose and relaxed. Now push the kettlebell through the legs. At first the participant will probably resist the movement and stop the kettlebell underneath them. Repeat the push and keep talking, cue with "relax the shoulders", at some stage the concept will be understood; this is when you can proceed to the next step.

(illustrated: pendulum concept drill)

It should be noted that 'the insert' is not part of the 'true pendulum concept', the pendulum concept is where the weight continues to swing freely, with the Cavemantraining teaching of the swing we promote an insert. Secondly, there is an active glute powered pull during the up phase of the swing. The pendulum concept is and should be used to get across the

Taco Fleur

concept that the shoulders should not be involved to power the swing.

KETTLEBELL SWING - PENDULUM CONCEPT

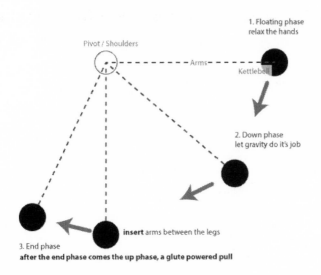

Kettlebell Insert

Here at Cavemantraining the Caveman Kettlebell swing has evolved over many years to make it the best it can be, involving as many muscle groups as possible and making it as safe as possible.

The kettlebell swing for fitness is an exercise that people perform to get results, those results are, but not limited to; building muscle; becoming stronger; becoming fitter, and to reach those goals you want to create as much resistance as you can while increasing the weight lifted, after all, it's resistance training!

Cavemantraining has added an optional 'insert' to the kettlebell swing, this partly breaks away from the common full pendulum concept which can sometimes create trajectory issues, especially with people who just started working with a kettlebell. What does the insert accomplish? The added insert prevents the kettlebell from bobbing at the end phase creating friction in the hands and hitting the kettlebell in the tailbone. A full pendulum ides the kettlebell upwards at the back swing, because the kettlebell travels through the gs there is only so far it can travel, this is due to the arms eventually being stopped ruptly by the legs/groin, therefor, an insert is safer and more comfortable. And last but t least, the insert taxes the trapezius muscle more by guiding the force of the kettlebell ck and towards the ground, thus creating a larger opposing force for the trapezius uscle group.

llowing is the kettlebell swing with insert broken down.

oating phase

- Almost all muscles involved in the movement are contracted
- Wait for gravity to take control of the kettlebell
- The grip on the handle is relaxed
- The kettlebell is comes to about chest or shoulder height

Taco Fleur

Down phase / partial pendulum

- Wait for the right moment to break at the hips and start pulling them back
- If you break to early then the kettlebell comes out of the trajectory
- Activate the gluteus maximus slightly to absorb some of downward pulling force
- Gently relax the gluteus maximus to control the hip hinge movement
- Activate the lattisimus dorsi and pull them down to keep the shoulders in th sockets
- Activate the erector spinae to keep the spine neutral
- At some stage the hips will have reached the furthest point backwards
- The kettlebell arrives near the legs

Down phase / insert

- Insert the arms between the legs by bringing the torso down more and guide th kettlebell towards the back, the swing is no longer a full pendulum
- Activate the trapezius to help absorb the deceleration which is about the take place
- Start decelerating the kettlebell

End phase

- The kettlebell is at the furthest point it should go through the legs and is ready to b pulled back up

Up phase / powering

- Squeeze the gluteus maximus to power the hip hinge which initiates the coming upright of the body
- First part of the up-phase should be pulling out which is directing the force diagonally
- Second part is standing up, pushing the feet into the ground and directing the force

vertically

- Although it might look like your focussing on pushing the hips forward, you're actually focussing on standing up right, transferring power from lower-body to upper-body
- If you stand up too early, then the weight becomes unbalanced and the toes will likely come off the ground

rip

- During the down phase the grip will tighten, but only as much as is required
- During the end phase the grip is the tightest
- During the up phase the grip starts to relax
- During the floating phase the grip is the most relaxed

rms

he arms should follow the kettlebell at all times, think of the kettlebell as an extension of he arms, from side-on view you want to see the kettlebell inline with the arms at all times. the bell starts to droop, then the swing is not powered by the posterior chain, and the houlders will be doing the work

Taco Fleur

Illustrated: drooping kettlebell

Hamstrings

You should feel a stretch on your hamstrings on each repetition of the swing (down / end phase).

Why the Insert?

- To prevent the bell from bobbing
- To prevent the arms from being stopped abruptly by the legs if the pendulum motion had continued
- To guide the kettlebell towards the ground and create an opposing force for the trapezius muscle group (adding more resistance for the muscle group)
- To provide an increased stretch for the hamstrings

Taco Flex

t should be noted that each repetition of the kettlebell swing isn ·hanges as you fatigue, your mind starts to drift, you get lazy or try 1ot expected to perform the same swing every-time, as long as it · owards your goals it's okay.

peed changes during your swings, if you're doing high volume you'll be working slower, if /ou're doing low volume you might be working faster, however, speed should never change o grinding. As you fatigue you might delay the timing of the hip hinge and so on, the objective of our education is to provide you with the why's and understanding reasons for loing one thing over the other and then it's up to you to implement the right technique for /our moment in time.

Explosiveness

The Squat Jump drill is a great way to develop the explosiveness required with the napping of the hips. You'll find that most people who just started swinging a kettlebell and re used to doing hip hinge deadlifts will perform the swing too slow. They'll use more of he upper-body to power the move due to the lack of explosiveness. Ask the participant to oring the hands to the chest, come into a semi-squatting position (half hip hinge, half quat). Have her or him jump high up in the air, with the body being straight in the air but anding with knees bend to absorb the impact. You will have to explain that this drill is only done to experience the explosiveness required for the swing, it's not the movement pattern itself which requires attention.

(illustrated: squat jump drill)

Taco Fleur

...k drill is great way to teach someone what the top position of the swing should feel and what muscles should be engaged. The high plank is performed by

- First kneeling on the floor
- Placing your hands directly under your shoulders with elbows locked out
- Pushing your chest out
- Pulling the shoulders back and down with the lats
- Engaging the rhomboids to slightly pull the shoulder blades in
- Engaging your abdominals like someone is going to punch you in the stomach
- Locking out the knees
- Activating the quads and squeezing the glutes while lifting your knees of the ground and coming into a high plank position where only your hands and toes are on the ground
- Your whole body is perfectly aligned

Illustrated: high plank, initial position

Taco Fleur

Illustrated: high plank

Note that this is also a great way to test core strength. A weak core will affect posture and hip hinging ability with added resistance.

Height of the Swing

The height that the Kettlebell should end up in is not set in stone. A good height to aim for is chest or shoulder height, but if the Kettlebell does not travel that high or travels slightly further, that is certainly not bad. It's important to make this point clear as people will want to start pulling the kettlebell higher with the shoulders, promote more glute power, squeezing, snapping and pushing into the ground, refer back to the squat jump drill.

In competitions or challenges the minimum height is generally shoulder height; it's an easy standard to measure and clear to see from the side. The heavier the Kettlebell gets, the more effort is required to get it to chest height. Thus if you notice a client or yourself swinging each rep higher than chest height you might want to increase weight.

The American Swing goes all the way above the head. Good range of motion in the shoulders is required before attempting to swing the kettlebell that high. There is a lot of

Taco Fleur

controversy between the American and Russian Swing, don't get caught up in the war! Both the American and Russian Swing are equally good in the right context***.

Breathing

There are different breathing techniques for the swing; you should explore which one works best for you. The most common one is inhaling through the nose on the down phase and exhaling through the mouth on the up phase while keeping the abdominal muscles tight and firm. The kettlebell sport swing promotes exhaling on the down-phase and in on the up-phase.

Timing

Correct timing is extremely important with the swing. You have to get familiar with the movement; some aspects remain the same across all variables while others change, depending on weight, height of swing, and the participant. Practicing will allow you to master the art of timing.

Calluses and Hand Maintenance

Calluses are a thickened layer of skin that can develop on your hands when working with Kettlebells. It's a layer of dead skin which is caused by friction between the handle and the skin. To keep the development of calluses to a minimum, make sure the handle of the kettlebell is not moving within your grip during the swing (i.e. bobbing at the end phase of the swing) and that you're not gripping it too tight.

It is important to maintain your hands when calluses do develop. Unmaintained calluses can turn into ripped calluses, untreated or ripped calluses are painful. They can become infected and take you out of action for a while. If your calluses tear during a workout, it is recommend to immediately treat it with an antibacterial solution and bandage it.

You should shave or peel your calluses regularly and apply moisturiser to the area. A good tool to use for maintaining calluses is a Scraper, File or Pumice Stone.

Soak your hands for a few minutes in warm water for a few minutes and then use the Pumice Stone to treat the areas, if you soaked long enough, the callused areas will look white.

Chalk

When you do lots of swings, your palms will probably start to sweat and your grip on the Kettlebell becomes slippery. This is not good, as the Kettlebell can potentially slip out of your hands. It can also produce blisters and require you to start employing a tighter grip. To avoid this, you can use chalk. Chalk is great—it can also help with reducing the development of calluses—but don't overdo it or it can have the opposite effect. Use chalk sparingly, just enough to lightly cover the effected parts of your hands, and rub a little on the Kettlebell handle. If you start seeing clumps of chalk on your hands, you've used too much. Reapply when your hands start getting sweaty and slippery again.

Gloves

The use of gloves with Kettlebell training is not recommended. It removes the connection between you and the Kettlebell which removes the sensory connection from the hand to the brain. You won't learn to employ the correct grips, you'll get lazy about gripping technique and won't develop the grip strength that comes as an added benefit of Kettlebell training. Gloves can bunch up and make the grip uncomfortable. You won't develop any calluses at all using gloves. This may sound good, but in reality you should be developing moderate calluses when working with Kettlebells and maintain those.

Footwear

Training with bare feet is the most effective way to train with Kettlebells. It's great for developing stability and muscle strength in the feet. The next best thing for footwear is five finger shoes or shoes with a flat sole.

Running shoes or shoes with a thick sole take away the connection between your body and the floor; they will potentially cause instability and ankle issues. They can also cause 'happy feet' (moving feet) and other instability issues. More importantly, with thick soled shoes you're losing power generated by the lower body. A solid grounding will allow you to use all the power you can generate from the lower-body. Running shoes are great for running, but not for Kettlebell training, where the weight constantly shifts around the body and a solid connection with the ground is required to accommodate and anticipate this constant shifting of weight.

Note that there is a whole lot more than can be said about training bare feet and these few paragraphs don't do it justice. I highly recommend doing further research on the Internet, or look up my article[†] online about training with bare feet.

Quality over Quantity

When you initially start Kettlebell Training or doing the Kettlebell Swing, you should focus

Taco Fleur

on quality rather than quantity. In other words, rather than doing 50 swings with incorrect technique, do 5 sets of 10, or 10 sets of 5 where the focus is on thinking about every point raised within this document.

Grow Gradually

It's impossible to execute everything that is mentioned within this document perfectly your first time. Perhaps not even over a period of six months, maybe not even within a year if you're not training regularly and constantly focusing on every point made in this document.

The most important things to focus on initially are the safety points. Understand and execute those, and then start adding the next points raised, those points that will make your technique more efficient and allow you to swing more weight.

Take it step by step, create your own plan, take the points that you currently understand, write them down and work on those. Once you feel you have a good understanding of them, read the document again, write down some more points you want to focus on. Grow gradually until you've mastered the swing technique.

Choosing Weight

It is important that you start swinging with the right weight. If you pick a weight too light, you don't get the resistance you need for activating the right muscles. Pick a weight too heavy and your form will go out the door.

As a general rule, and keeping in mind everyone is different, use a 6kg Kettlebell for a child, and start women on 8kg at least.

Start men out with at least 10 or 12kg Kettlebells. Always make sure to assess your clients' swing from side and front-on. If form goes out the door with these weights, reset, go through the exercise and drills again making sure the client understands what muscles to activate rather than moving down in weight—a common mistake.

Common Sense

Every human being is built differently. It's important to keep in mind that certain moves, cues, or tips might not work the same for your body. Always use common sense and adjust the exercise to your body.

As long as the exercise is performed safely, any slight adjustments should be fine. If unsure, visit the World Kettlebell Community forum on http://kettlebells.community and ask your question under "The Kettlebell Swing".

The Movement Step by Step

> Stand in spine-neutral position with feet slightly wider than shoulder-width apart with the Kettlebell in-front of you.

> Hip hinge and hold the Kettlebell by the handle with both hands and a loose grip. The handle should rest in the fingers rather than the palm, make sure not to employ a crush grip.

 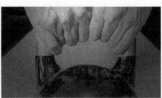 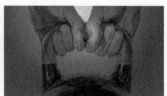

Illustrated: hip hinge, grip with pinkies in and out

> There are two ways to start the swing, you can start with a Dead Swing or Deadlift and Leg Bump. You're going to start with the Dead Swing by pulling the Kettlebell off the ground and between the legs.

> Keep your feet flat on the ground at all times to be able to push into the ground and activate the hamstring muscles. Snap the hips forward and bring the body upright to power the movement. Transfer the power from lower to upper body during the up phase.

> After the floating phase you break at the hips and push them back; try and keep the knees directly over the ankles as much as possible (shins vertical). You should feel tension on the hamstrings when pushing the hips back. Remember that this is not a squat. Note that the point of breaking at the hips all depends on where the Kettlebell is; in some cases the height of the Kettlebell might be such that you need to wait a fraction of a second before breaking at the hips, other times it might be that you need to break the moment the Kettlebell starts falling. The timing is something you will need to work on and perfect over time while keeping all safety tips in mind.

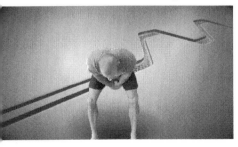

> Do not involve your shoulders to lift the Kettlebell upwards, let the force from the pushing of the hips and the coming upright of the body propel the Kettlebell. Note

Taco Fleur

that with the American Swing the shoulders are involved, and will pull the Kettlebell further up till positioned above the head.

> The Kettlebell should come through the legs approximately around the knees, you should be able to put another Kettlebell between your legs and not hit it.

> Elbows and forearms should be making contact around the waist line. Part of the wrists should contact around the upper thighs. Think about 'inserting' your arms between your legs.

> The top of the swing is when the Kettlebell is motionless for a split second. Relax your grip at this point. The Kettlebell usually reaches about chest height but keep in mind that the Kettlebell only needs to swing as high as the force generated by your hips will move it.

Taco Fleur

> When the Kettlebell starts to fall down, it's time to start thinking about breaking at the hips and tighten the grip on the handle bit by bit, but only as little as is required.

> Squeeze the glutes (gluteus maximus) when bringing the hips forward. The torso should follow the hips and not vice versa. In other words, the hips should lead and the torso should follow.

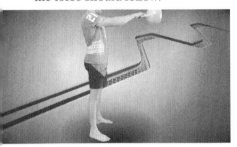

> Maintain a neutral spine at all times, with the only exception being during the down phase, when the head can be slightly tilted up if you're having trouble keeping your shoulders back and chest out. Otherwise your head should remain in line with your torso at all times to avoid neck strain.

> Stand up straight with muscles engaged like in the plank position. Do not hyperextend the back when snapping the hips forward. That is, do not push your hips past your ankles and shoulders.

Taco Fleur

> During the down phase there is a stage where the hips can't go any further, the torso will continue to come down to guide the kettlebell towards the back, to decelerate and to prevent the Kettlebell from bobbing.

> At the top of the swing remember:
>   ☐ chest out and shoulders back
>   ☐ engage the core
>   ☐ squeeze the glutes
>   ☐ legs are straight
>   ☐ hands can relax the grip more to give the muscles a break

> Guide the kettlebell towards the back of you, prevent it from swinging upwards to where it can't go and the arms will stop but the kettlebell will want to go further and start bobbing.

Taco Fleur

- You can immediately pull the kettlebell back up once it hits the furthest point through the legs. This adds the most resistance.

- The alternative is to wait for it to start swinging back and then pull up. This is more like the sport style swing, has less resistance and is more efficient. If you start doing high volume repetitions, you're better off choosing this style.

- Leave the arms relaxed but straight at all times—elbows can be locked out or not—and only use the arms as a pendulum so the Kettlebell can swing freely.

- Pull the lats down, not only to add another muscle group to the exercise, but also to keep the shoulders nicely positioned within their sockets. The added benefit is more control on the up and down phase.

Faults and Correction

Hyper Extending the Back

This is usually done to get the kettlebell up higher.

Correction: Remind the participant about the plank, promote more hip drive, put your hand at the hyper extension point and ask for it not to be touched.

Happy Feet

The feet are moving around or partially coming off the floor. This is usually caused by improper weight distribution (i.e., the weight is coming too far forward or back) and the feet are not pushed flat into the ground.

Correction: Remind the participant about the Squat Jump. Ask him or her to push his or her feet into the ground like he or she is going to jump. Happy feet can also prevent the participant from being able to activate the right muscles.

Frontal Raise

he shoulders are pulling the Kettlebell up rather than the hip drive powering the swing; ou can also see that the Kettlebell starts to droop, rather than being in line with the arms.

Correction: Remind the participant about the pendulum, promote more hip drive, if eed be, stop the participant and get them to do the Pendulum or Squat Jump drill.

Kettlebell Coming too Low

he kettlebell is coming too low to the ground when passing through the legs. This can be aused by the participant not engaging their core muscles (being lazy), having weak core nuscles, the weight being too heavy, or it is related to proprioception issues, where the articipant simply does not have a good sense of the relative position of neighbouring parts f the body and strength of effort needing to be employed in the movement.

Correction: Remind the participant to come through between the legs with the Kettlebell t approximately knee height. After several failed attempts, you can put another Kettlebell between the legs and caution the participant about hitting it. Also, improve core strength and/or go down in weight.

Rounded Back

The participant has a rounded back rather than a neutral spine. This could be due to the weight being too heavy, not activating the right muscles, or having weak back muscles. Having a rounded back can cause strain on the muscles, tendons, and ligaments of the back, which in turn can lead to discomfort or serious injury. A neutral or correctly aligned spine allows the skeletal system to safely take some load of the muscles.

Correction: Ask the participant to push out her or his chest, activate the lats, and slightly squeeze the shoulder blades together. If the cues do not provide a fix, stop and ask the participant to go into a plank and make the corrections step by step.

Kettlebell Bobbing

The Kettlebell makes a quick, short movement up and down at the end of the backswing. This can potentially punch the participant in the buttocks or cause friction in the palms. The bobbing is usually caused by improper guidance of the Kettlebell, pulling back to early, or the torso not coming down enough.

Correction: Explain the path in which the Kettlebell should be guided by the participant or ask the participant to come down towards the ground more with the torso. Another way to get the participant down more is to ask him or her to follow the Kettlebell with one's eyes until they see the ground (head remains in line with torso). Last resort: stop them, remove the Kettlebell, and ask them to perform a bodyweight Hip Hinge and stop in the hang phase. Repeat several times and ask them to feel the position and pay attention to the angles.

Cowboy Legs

The feet are placed too close together, not allowing enough space for the Kettlebell to travel through the legs. The participant will need to pull the knees outwards to allow the Kettlebell to travel through; doing this will cause unnecessary stress on the knees and also prevent proper muscle activation.

Correction: Ask the participant to place their feet wider apart. Stop if need be, and put participant in the static hang phase of the hip hinge, with proper feet placement, and push the Kettlebell through the legs a few times, so the participant can experience the feeling.

Torso Coming too Low

The participant comes too low with the torso. This is usually because the eyes are following the kettlebell, while they should stop approximately just before seeing the ground underneath. They should not follow the kettlebell through the legs.

Correction: Point at where you expect the eyes to stop following the Kettlebell. If this does not help, put an object at the point where you want the eyes to stop following the Kettlebell.

Knees Staying Bent

The participant is not standing up straight, and the knees remain bent during each rep. This will cause the participant to lose power generated by the legs. The cause is usually fatigue, but can also be laziness.

Taco Fleur

Correction: Ask the participant to press the floor and stand up straight. Remind the participant about the plank. Next, ask the participant to start locking out the knees, if this does not improve the issue, then suggest rest.

Feet too Far Apart

The participant has their feet too far apart, almost looking like a sumo squat. This will reduce the power generated by the snapping of the hips. It will also make it difficult for the arms to connect with the thighs.

Correction: Ask the participant to bring her or his feet closer together.

Power Swinging

Although this swing style actually exists, the conventional swing should be mastered first. If programming calls for a conventional swing, this is what should be performed.

You can spot a Power Swing when the participant is not guiding the kettlebell but pushing it down and/or pulling it up to increase the speed of the swing.

Correction: Ask the participant to simply let gravity take control, just think about guiding the Kettlebell where it should go.

Aches and Pains

Some of the most common aches and pains—further referred to as issues—caused by incorrect technique are listed below.

Lower Back

The following can be potential causes for lower back issues:

- No activation of the gluteus maximus and pulling the Kettlebell up with the lower back muscles

- Too many repetitions
- Weight being too heavy

Forearms

The following can be potential causes for forearm issues:

- Grip on the Kettlebell too tight
- Too many repetitions and not enough rest
- Not relaxing grip at the top of the swing

Elbow / Upper arms

The following can be potential causes for upper arm issues:

- Elbows remain bent causing stress on the biceps
- Swinging too heavy
- Performing high reps while unconditioned

Shoulders

The following can be potential causes for shoulder (deltoids) issues:

- Pulling the kettlebell up
- Not pushing the chest out and shoulders back
- Not pulling the lats down

Knees

The following can be potential causes for knee issues:

Taco Fleur

- Hyperextending the knees
- Cowboy legs
- Knees collapsing in on the down phase
- Squatting (incorrect squat movement) rather than hinging
- Sumo stance, too wide with the feet apart

Cues

Common cues for teaching are:

- Relax the shoulders
- Chest out
- Pull the lats down
- Shoulders back
- Scapulae pulled down
- Neutral spine or straight back
- More explosive
- Pull the knees back
- Shins vertical
- Don't turn it into a squat
- Feel the tension on the hamstrings
- Pull the hips back more
- Active core
- Lock the elbows out
- Straight arms
- Guide the kettlebell towards the back
- Control your breathing
- Keep the feet flat
- Push into the ground

To fix out of sync movement, you can clap your hands when the participant should for example be snapping the hips. You can choose to gently slap the participant on the amstrings at the moment he or she should be exploding the hips forward. Do make sure ou ask for permission before touching a participant.

o make sure the participant engages their abdominals, you can choose to gently slap the articipant in the areas they should pay attention to once they're in the up phase of the wing.

- Become a certified Caveman Kettlebell Trainer and complete the course online‡ -

Notes

ocking out: If you're not familiar with the movement yet and feel like you still have a lot o learn, play it safe and keep the knees soft. If you're confident that you can lock your oints with care and you feel like your posture and power improves when doing so, then mplement this technique.

What's Next?

his book focussed on one thing only, the double-arm conventional kettlebell swing hip inge style, now that you know the ins and outs, your next step should be to perfect the this wing, it's variations and then move on to the single-arm swing, snatching and other ettlebell training exercises.

* Amazon Ebook http://amzn.to/1Vndww7

** Cavemantraining Ebook plus Audiobook http://bit.ly/23LSPid

*** Squatting vs Hip Hinging article http://bit.ly/1VoAseK

**** American vs Russian Swing article http://bit.ly/1SUsYcB

† Training bare feet article http://bit.ly/23LSEDB

‡ Online Kettlebell Course http://bit.ly/1Mxq63k

Personal Note

I like to connect with people who have read this ebook, add me on Facebook, Google+ or LinkedIn. Please consider leaving a review on Amazon and join the Kettlebell Swing group (see below).

https://www.facebook.com/taco.fleur

https://plus.google.com/+TacoFleur

https://www.linkedin.com/in/tacofleur

Taco Fleur

I've made an older version of this book available as a free online video, you can find the video on Youtube here https://www.youtube.com/watch?v=KC-wO9Gog1A please be aware that some of the explanation has changed over time, however, this book will always have the most up to date version.

This content is part of an online kettlebell course on http://kettlebelltraining.education

Subscribe to the Cavemantraining Youtube channel for regular kettlebell videos
youtube.com/channel/UCBRlDOmwDoptO7LrdlUhsog

Join www.cavemantraining.com for regular free workouts

Join us for discussion in the Kettlebell Swing group on Facebook
https://www.facebook.com/groups/kettlebell.swing/

Taco Fleur